# ERLING HA,

*THE INSPIRATIONAL STORY OF THE WORLD'S PREMIER FORWARD*

By

*JACKSON CARTER*

Copyright © 2021

# TABLE OF CONTENTS

## LEGAL NOTES

Erling Haaland is meant for entertainment and educational use only. All attempts have been made to present factual information in an unbiased context.

# EARLY LIFE

Erling Braut Haaland, the Golden Boy of modern-day football is on his way to astronomical heights. Ever since he broke into the Bundesliga with Borussia Dortmund, there is hardly a top-flight team that hasn't enquired about the young Norwegian or is keen for his signature. Yet, it isn't the first time we've heard this name "Haaland," as many Premier League enthusiasts can still remember a certain Alf-Inge Haaland and his face-off with Roy Keane!

Erling Braut Haaland was born on the 21st of July 2000 in Leeds, England. Although a Norwegian international, Haaland was born in Leeds because his father, Alf-Inge Haaland, represented the infamous white jersey of Leeds United. Alf-Inge Haaland was a defensive midfielder, often placed between the two positions. He spent a decade in the English top-flight racking up appearances for the likes of Nottingham Forest where he made his Premier League debut in 1993. Although his arrival was supposed to be a year prior under the management of Brian Clough in 1992, the transfer was completed in 1993 under Frank Clark. Alf-Inge Haaland made his debut against Leicester City. Previously, he had spent 3 years in his hometown club, Bryne FK, before making the big move. His presence on the pitch was mostly on the defensive half, but he managed to score 4 times with Bryne FK in his 68 appearances. Alf-Inge Haaland later spent 4 seasons with the Forest, making 75 appearances in all competitions and scoring 7 goals. He helped Nottingham Forest place third in the league and qualify for the UEFA Cup or now more commonly known as the Europa League.

In the summer of 1997, he made a move to Leeds United under the then Scottish Manager, George Graham. His debut for the Peacocks came against a formidable foe, Arsenal, on 9th August 1997. Just a month after his arrival to West Yorkshire, Alf-Inge Haaland made some serious headlines for both good and bad reasons. In September 1997, Leeds was one goal up in a game against Manchester United, which was scored by the Norwegian himself. The home battle for Leeds was daunting as ever since The Red Devils were a top team. Alf-Inge Haaland and Roy Keane were both tussling for the ball when Keane fell to the ground in pain and agony. Unbeknownst to Haaland, Roy Keane had suffered a fatal injury when his anterior cruciate ligament or ACL was torn. Haaland was completely unaware of the injury and Keane's reaction, as he had the impression that Keane went down to win a set piece. He later stood over Keane who was still very much rolling on the turf and criticized him for the ill-shaken diving act. In Haaland's defense, the contact and situation did not align to present a serious injury, and a fake attempt to gain a penalty would surely rile up any defender. However, that was not the case, as Roy Keane was stretchered off the field and Haaland was booked for his reactionary antics. Keane was out of football for nearly an entire year.

Haaland later scored a goal against Liverpool as Leeds lost the tie 1 - 3, with that one goal coming from the Norwegian on the 26th of November 1997. His son, Erling Braut Haaland, achieved the same feat nearly 22 years later on the 2nd of October 2019. Alf-Inge Haaland was also part of the Leeds Squad that made headlines by reaching the semi-finals of the UEFA Cup during the 1999-2000 season and also qualified for the UEFA Champions

League. Haaland served as a utility player, often placed at the defensive line or in the midfield by Coach David O'Leary.

Alf-Inge Haaland then made his final move in the Premier League when he signed for Manchester City for a 2.5 Million Pound fee in 2000. In April 2001, Manchester City was due to face Manchester United in the Derby. Roy Keane had made it back into the team and proceeded to lunge into Haaland as a form of revenge. The tackle was by no means clean, as he aimed high for the right knee. Keane was subsequently sent off for that challenge and faced a three-match ban in addition to a 5000-pound fine. Haaland later suffered a knock on his left knee and, despite surgery, could never regain full fitness. Therefore, he used a medical clause in his contract and stopped playing football as he was unable to physically. He did make a comeback 8 years later for Rosseland BK but would retire for good with 9 games played that season and a single goal.

Erling Braut Haaland, his son, had been transforming himself into the beast we all know today. Very well known for his big stature, blistering pace, athleticism, and strength, he is a threat to any defense. His playing style and overall physique are similar to that of Zlatan Ibrahimovic whom Haaland looks up to. His nickname "The Terminator" is a reflection of his accumulative abilities by his fans and admirers. Haaland was born in Leeds where his father was a first-team regular. They later moved to their hometown of Bryne where Haaland initially grew up. He was 3 at the time and started off his early life in his country just as his parents desired. From an early age, Haaland was very much intrigued by sports. Alongside his passion for football, he often took part in other sports such as Handball, Golf, and Track & Field, all of which have helped him grow into the athletic beast that he is at the moment. Haaland also allegedly achieved a world record in his age category, with a recorded distance of 1.69 meters in the standing long jump when he was just 5 years old in 2006. Erling was an energetic kid from the start, religiously playing football with his friends and showcasing high levels of confidence.

In 2006, Haaland was enrolled in a local club, Bryne Fotballklubb, where he established the desire to make it big and had the willpower and mentality to realize his goal.

# STARTING IN CLUB LEAGUE

After Haaland was initially made to play as a winger, Berntsen put him in his preferred central role as a striker after a few matches. Although he failed to score in his breakthrough season at Bryne, Haaland was offered a trial by the German club, 1899 Hoffenheim, before eventually moving to Molde FK to play under Ole Gunnar Solskjær. Haaland made a total of sixteen senior appearances for Bryne.

Erling Haaland started his club and league venture early on by joining his hometown youth club, Bryne Fotballklubb or Bryne FK. At the time he was enrolled in their program, Haaland was just 5 years old, and within a year of his enrollment, he decided to focus on football. A very bold act for a 6-year-old, he followed his statement by conceiving the thought of becoming the World's Best Player.

His former youth coach, Alf Yngve Berntsen, at Bryne FK spoke highly of him in an interview with Goal.com, stating:

"I saw Erling for the first time when he was five when he joined indoor training with a group one year older ... His first two touches led to goals. He was very, very good from the first moment, even though he hadn't played in the club before. He started playing in his own year group, but because he was so much better than the others, we immediately pulled him up to Under-6."

Bryne was a small-town club with not many resources like the top-flight clubs around Europe, however, Haaland was determined to fire through the ranks. He spent an entire decade with the club and would always survive the ax as underperforming players would be cut out of the team. Haaland was also known to play competitive games a year ahead of the curve from the age of 6 till 16.

His coach further stated in an interview with Bundesliga.com: "As he grew older, he was always hardworking, a really nice guy to work with. And he smiled a lot, trained a lot, and scored a lot. A guy like Erling, you can't create that. He's born with special gifts. No matter who we played against, he respected the opponents, but he was never afraid. That also, I think, is very important."

Haaland's raw ability and natural finishing blew him up through the ranks and his overall competitive instincts saw him achieve the senior-team status for Bryne FK at the tender age of 16. During the 2015 -2016 campaign, Haaland was an active part of the Bryne reserve team. He put in great performances and impressed the coaching staff. Erling Haaland had racked up a whopping 18 goals in just 14 matches, which was an insane statistic. The first team and club knew the potential he had and in May 2016, he earned his first-team debut.

The initial manager of the team, Gaute Larsen, was sacked from the managerial position and youth coach, Bernsten, who had already worked very closely with Haaland became the temporary manager. His arrival was pivotal to Haaland's entry into the first team. He was offered his first start a few months from his 16th birthday, meaning that Erling made the debut at just 15 years of age. The debut match was against the second-division side, Ranheim, on the 12th of May 2016. By the end of the 2015 - 2016 season, Haaland had made 16 appearances for the club, 12 of them from the bench and starting the other 4. During this time, he was advancing both at the club and international level. In 2016, Erling Haaland went from Norway's Under-15 side to the Under-17 side, a glimmer of hope for the Norwegian coaches as speculation arose regarding whether he would stick to his Father's country of birth or his own, which would've otherwise seen him join the England team.

Haaland was initially deployed out wide as a winger because of his blistering pace, but Bersten would later stick him in his preferred role of a central striker after examining his performances in the initial position. However, Haaland would fail to score at his starting season at Bryne. He made a total of 16 appearances for Bryne FK, failing to score a single goal. However, his ability and desire as a tall standing striker have been very sought after. Despite not scoring with the first team, he was a ruthless attacker with bags of potential. Those are the attributes top teams look for in a player. However, after his first-team appearances, the German Bundesliga club, Hoffenheim 1899, offered the young Norwegian a trial at their establishment. The trial and prerequisites were all in place and went well for both parties. Haaland had already showcased himself through his performances at Bryne FK's second team, where he scored 18 goals in 14 matches and later capped 16 times for the first team. Hoffenheim was very keen on the player—he was just 15 years old at the time and about to turn 16. He spent a week at their establishment undergoing evaluation. The youth team coaches were impressed, to say the least, and gave the green light to sign the youngster. However, the deal went sour as Hoffenheim didn't want to pay the 5000€ wage the player and his agents were asking for. The issue was in a shaky state, as the Hoffenheim 1899 club policy stated that all youth players should be paid the same wage/salary of 2000€. Haaland's representatives felt that this was a low ball for the immense talent of their client, and a pay cut of over 50% was not suitable. As a result, the deal collapsed and Hoffenheim ultimately pulled the plug on the transfer.

Soon after the transfer debacle with Hoffenheim, Haaland turned 16 years old. In 2017, Ole Gunnar Solskjær was the manager at Molde FK. He has had his eyes on the youngster and had been monitoring him for a while. Later in the same year, Ole Gunnar Solskjær decided to sign Erling Haaland. Ole Gunnar Solskjaer was also a former international teammate of Erling Haaland's father, Alfie Haaland. This connection, and because he is also a Norwegian, helped Ole to persuade Erling to join Molde in order to mold him into the club's future plan.

# Moving To Norway's Top League: Molde

With overflowing potential and a new stage to perform on, Erling Haaland was set for the Norwegian top flight, Eliteserien. He was always destined to play at the biggest level, and scooping him up from the divisions below proved to be very fruitful for then manager, Ole Gunnar Solskjaer. There was no doubt in Haaland's mind to leave his childhood club, Bryne, as his progression always showcased his ability to perform well. Therefore, when Molde Fk came knocking, a swift transfer session ensued. The manager Ole had a vast influence in bringing him to the club and the limelight as a prolific striker in his own era. Ole was aware of his talent and physical attributes as an attacker. Solskjaer himself was a rather scrawny striker, even though his father was a wrestling champion in the '60s. Ole had the understanding and therefore adapted his game to his physical strength, adjusting his game to be based on movement, finding the right opportunity, and clean finishing. Ole transformed himself into an elite striker and went on to win 6 premier league titles and the UCL competition in 1999 with Manchester United. With the former player and current prospect having similar attributes, Ole began the process of bringing him to Molde. Haaland was already a fast, ruthless, and quintessential box-to-box player, which had pushed through the ranks. With further refinement of his techniques and build, a potential monster was under the making. Haaland, therefore, followed a strict regimen and diet to help him grow. Soon, Haaland bulked up drastically unlike Ole in the past. With his newly formed strength and physique, Haaland was able to push off defenders while remaining a fast and potent threat in enemy lines.

"Some of my strengths I can see in Erling. But in other things, he's a lot better than me already, I can say that. I think maybe he's learned a few things from me, you know, mentality and stuff, the will to win," said Haaland Sr. to Bundesliga.com

Naturally blessed with a tall physique and strong mentality, Haaland packed 15 kg of complete muscle at Molde under Ole Gunnar Solskjær. This allowed him to compete in the tougher and more demanding first division. Soon after, he started racking up goals and appearances at Molde.

On February 1st, 2017, Haaland was officially announced by Molde FK. His first-ever appearance for the club came in the Norwegian Cup, where Molde was set to face Volda TI on the 26th of April 2017. Haaland's debut was very well received, as he scored to help Molde take a 3-2 win in the fixture, which was his debut and first-ever goal for the club. With a strong start to his career at Molde, the fans and management alike were invested in his talent and soon enough, on the 4th of June 2017, Haaland was due to make his debut in the Eliteserien. The fixture was against Sarpsborg FK, but both teams drew 0 - 0. Ole Gunnar Solskjaer was determined to get a goal, so he signaled for Haaland to start warming up. In the 71st minute of the match, he came on as a substitute. Within a minute of his debut, Haaland was penalized and given a yellow card, not the start he planned but it got better. Haaland received the ball in the 77th minute and scored his first goal for the club. The goal was the match-winner.

During the mid-season, on the 8th of August, Haaland's Molde FK faced off against Tromso in the Eliteserien. Erling did not start the match but was on the bench available for substitution. Tromso came into week 18 of the league with better form than the away side, Molde, winning 3 of their last 5 games and drawing the remaining 2. The home side, Tromso, took the lead in the 25th minute courtesy of their main striker, Olsen. Molde swiftly responded with a goal in the 27th minute through their own star striker, Svendsen. The game heated up till the half-time whistle. Brustad was replaced in the 70th Minute, as Erling Haaland came on as a substitute. With the game still a draw, Ole's side pressed high to get the next goal. With almost the entire team upfront around the 77th-minute mark, Hestad put in a lofted ball over the defender to the towering head of Erling Haaland who headed the ball onto the ground and into the goal! Molde were now 1 - 2 up courtesy of the future Golden Boy. The match ended, with Haaland securing yet another match-winner for his new club even as a substitute.

As a young prospect, Haaland was not given much playing time compared to the other starters. He was often subbed mid-game and would start in certain cases. His second goal for the club came a few months later when Molde FK faced the Viking FK on the 17th of September 2017. Molde FK was leading 2-1 when Fredrik Brustad was subbed off for Erling Haaland in the 64th minute. To Ole's dismay, the Vikings equalized in the 77th minute, bringing the score to a 2-2 standstill. Minutes after the conceded goal, Molde held up possession and placed a beautiful pass over the defensive line to F. Aursnes who then squared the ball to Erling Haaland. He neatly tucked the ball in the bottom left corner, winning the match for Molde in the 80th minute.

His goal proved decisive as the match ended in favor of the Tornekrattet. Haaland proceeded to celebrate his match-winner in front of Viking supporters after scoring the goal. This act, although harmless and fueled with passion, was criticized by his Icelandic teammate, Björn Bergmann Sigurðarson who felt that it was wrong for him to do so. Nonetheless, Haaland ended his debut season with 4 goals, from which he scored 2 in the Eliteserien and 2 in the Norwegian Cup. He made a total of 19 appearances in the season from which he started in three league games, coming off the bench 10 times in the league. In the Norwegian cup competition, he made 6 appearances, starting in two and coming on as a substitute four times.

Molde Fk ended the season as the runner-up in the Eliteserien, missing out on the top spot to Rosenberg by a 7-point margin. The team qualified for the Europa League and would play in the qualifying round in the upcoming season. As for Molde's run in the Norwegian cup, they pushed through to the semifinal of the cup before being thrashed 0 - 3 at home by Lillestrom. It was a season that saw them close to silverware, but they missed out in the final stages. The club ended their 10th consecutive year in the Norwegian top flight of Eliteserien placed second on the leaderboard. The team recorded 16 wins, 6 draws, and 8 defeats in the 2017 campaign.

For Molde FK, the 2018 Season was their 48th campaign in the Norwegian top-flight league and their 11th consecutive campaign following the name change to Eliteserien. Haaland and Molde were set to play in 3 competitions in this campaign: the league, the Norwegian Cup, and the UEFA Europa League for which they had qualified the season prior. Haaland had already spent a substantial amount of time with his teammates and was starting to adapt to the team's playing style. This greatly increased his confidence in the top flight of Norwegian football. The first league game for Molde Fk came on the 11th of March 2018 in a home game against Sandefjord. Haaland was not present in the match and they went on to thrash the opponents 5 - 0 to kick off their season in high spirits.

Erling soon made it back into the lineup. Out of the first 5 games of the season, Molde won 4 and lost 1. On the 5th match day, against a familiar side, Lillestrom Sk, Haaland scored his first goal of the season. Molde was awarded a penalty in the 41st minute of the game and Erling Haaland stood up to take it. The whistle blew and the Terminator struck the ball with his left foot straight into the top right-hand corner—a stunning penalty full of vigor and power. The penalty kick was his first goal from the spot and the equalizer Molde was hoping for right before the halftime whistle. Molde later went on to win the match 2-1, further moving up in the league table. Haaland proceeded to score his second of the season against Sarpsborg 08 on the 7th of May 2018. The match day 8 saw the visitors concede an early goal in the first minute of the game, but with quick pressing and a swift attack in the 8th minute, Haaland rose to the occasion. Quite literally, Haaland scored an amazing acrobatic scissors-kick finish to equalize the match for Molde FK. The match finished 2-2, forcing each team to take home a point.

Erling Haaland then played in and out of the team on a regular basis, but wouldn't get his third goal until the 1st of July 2018. On match day 15, in an away game to Brann at their home stadium, Brann Stadion in Bergen, Haaland was set loose. He managed to score 4 back-to-back goals within the first 21 minutes of the game, which demolished their opponent even before the halftime whistle. For the first goal in the 4th minute of the game, Haaland received a headed through ball, for which he used his lightning pace to outrun two defenders and skim the keeper who was off his line to knock the ball in the back of the net. With an early 1-0 lead, an audacious long ball by Hested in the 13th minute saw Haaland break forward before cutting the sole defender marking him, beating him for pace, and slotting it past the keeper to make it 2-0 and 2 goals for Haaland on the day. A defensive error in the 15th minute allowed Haaland to freely run past the defensive line, cut the keeper, and complete his hat-trick with a low finish toward the bottom left corner. His first-ever hat-trick for the club and his 5th overall goal of the season, Haaland and Molde weren't done yet, as a penalty kick in the 21st minute, converted by none other than Erling Braut Haaland himself, made it 4 on the day and his sixth goal overall. After the big win and the young superstar's immense performance, Ole Gunnar Solksjaer compared Haaland's playing style to that of Romelu Lukaku and also revealed that he had rejected several bids from various clubs looking to get the striker on board. Exactly a week later, on the 8th of July against Valerenga at home, Haaland continued his goalscoring prowess and bagged a brace as Molde went on to win the match 5-1. It was yet another huge win for then manager, Ole Gunnar Solskjaer. Haaland scored a fairly easy tap-in setup by the opponent. He then scored by nutmegging the keeper in a cheeky goal attempt.

In addition to upholding his goal count in the league, Haaland opened his European account by scoring a penalty against KF Laci in the Europa League qualifying round on the 26th of July 2018. This was his first-ever UEFA Competition goal and the first of many. Molde FK advanced in the competition with a 3-0 win in that round. He kept on adding to his league goal tally, as a converted penalty in the reverse fixture against Brann brought his tally up to 9 league goals. Haaland then went on a goalscoring spree, scoring yet another goal against Hibernian FC in the UEFA Europa League. He made it 16th on the 20th of October 2018 against Sarpsborg 08. Haaland would then suffer a sprained ankle injury, which prevented him from completing the remaining 3 games of the season, all of which Molde won. With his contributions as an amazing striker, Haaland had 16 goals for Molde in 30 games across all competitions. His goal tally made him Molde's top scorer in that season. And for his effort at Molde in the 2018 Eliteserien, he received the Eliteserien Breakthrough of the Year award, which signified his importance in the team's success that season and overall individual growth. Molde finished their campaign in second place as runner-up yet again with only a 5-point gap between them and the first-placed Rosenborg. They were eliminated from the Norwegian Cup early on as they suffered a defeat to Brattvag in the second round of the cup. As for the UEFA Europa League, they were eliminated by Zenit Saint Petersburg by 1 goal on aggregate in the playoff round.

# Going International: Red Bull Salzburg

With an outstanding performance in Norway with Molde FK, Erling Haaland was shaping up to be one hot footballing prospect. He had now scored 14 goals for Molde in 39 games, most of which he scored by coming off the bench and making an instant impact. His profound ability in terms of pace, positioning, and technicality made him a potent striker to be put up against. Overall, in his career, Haaland had scored 53 goals in 111 games for both club and country, an amazing record for an 18-year-old. Although Molde had brought him to the limelight and helped him maintain a progressive tempo, his stay at the club was never evident. Meant for greater competition and status, Erling Haaland the Norwegian wonder boy was set to leave his homeland. Although big offers from Juventus and Bayern Leverkusen came about, Erling did not entertain them as, in his view, they were potentially disastrous deals. His thought process behind his decision to move to an entirely different club was to gain more playing time rather than make more money, which would later help him showcase more of his abilities and help secure his dream move. Thus, he disregarded offers from super big clubs and signed with Red Bull Salzburg, which had the perfect environment that could help shape his journey to fame. In August of 2018, Erling Braut Haaland left Molde to join RB Salzburg.

On the 19th of August 2019, Red Bull Salzburg, the reigning champions of the Austrian Bundesliga, announced that Erling Braut Haaland would be joining the club for an undisclosed fee. He arrived at the club on the 1st of January 2019 under a lucrative 5-year contract with the

Red Bull giants. The move to Red Bull Salzburg was very well thought out by Haaland, as his performances could easily get him transferred to Red Bull Leipzig the parent club of Red Bull Salzburg. Haaland's presence was not all that needed at the club, as their current striker, Mu'nas Dabbur, had been banging in goals consistently. RB Salzburg realized the potential and capabilities of Haaland, noting that it only makes sense to have him on board. That decision turned out to be very fruitful, as Haaland adapted very well to the game and at a progressive pace. The Austrian giants were on top of their game, having won 9 consecutive titles in the Austrian Bundesliga. Reports stated that before Haaland signed officially for Red Bull Salzburg, Erling had been approached by Leeds United, the hometown club of the city he was born in. Haaland has never shied away from admitting his allegiance to the club and has publicly stated that he supports them. However, the deal did not go through. No one has information regarding the reasons he didn't sign with them and the offer made to him, but it is obvious that Haaland would not have accepted given the importance and the type of offer Red Bull Salzburg made to him. Thus, when the deal was finalized, Erling Braut Haaland moved to Austria to compete in their version of the Bundesliga.

In his first season with his new club, Erling Haaland played only 5 games in all competitions. His only goal came against LASK in the Austrian Bundesliga. At the home game in Red Bull Arena on the 12th of May 2019, Haaland scored his first goal for the club by calmly finishing a lobbed ball from deep. His positioning was immense during his first goal, which had caught out LASK's entire backline with one swift motion, a glimpse of what he was capable of. He played only one game in all competitions from the cup to the UEFA Champions League. With minimal game time, he could not conjure up a goal. However, the upcoming season would reveal his true potential.

On the 19th of July 2019, Erling Braut Haaland scored his first-ever hat-trick for the Austrian club, finishing off their opponent, SC-ESV Parndorf, 7 - 1 in the Austrian Cup. He started off his scoring by converting a penalty in the 34th minute, which would open his scoring account for the season. The second goal came when an RB Salzburg free-kick was rebounded by the keeper right onto Haaland's feet, who simply tucked the ball away to complete his brace in the 73rd minute. A quick counterattack from the team opened up the defense. Haaland ran across the backside and thumped the ball with sheer ferocity to complete his hat-trick and close the scoring for the match, which ended 7 - 1. His first goal in the Austrian Bundesliga came about when Red Bull Salzburg faced Mattersburg at home on the 4th of August 2019. Haaland converted a penalty in the 37th minute by placing it in the bottom left corner, sending the keeper the wrong way, and putting Salzburg 3 goals up. His league goal tally was just getting started, as, a week after his first Bundesliga goal, RB Salzburg was due to face Wolfsberger on the 10th of August 2019. He started off his scoring in the 22nd minute by converting an uncleared and bubbling ball to put the team ahead. His second goal came in the second half in the 56th minute. A decent hold-up play allowed Haaland to make a run in from behind past the keeper before scoring his second goal of the game. Haaland dribbled the ball away from 3 defenders before having a quick one-two with a teammate, nutmegging the keeper to complete his first-ever Austrian Bundesliga hat-trick. The game ended 5 -2 for the home side as Wolfsberger suffered a loss.

A week later, on the 4th match day of the season, Haaland was back on the score sheet after scoring a brace against SKN St. Polten in a thrashing win over their opponent. The game ended 6 - 0 in favor of Salzburg. He scored his first goal in his signature style by moving the ball over to his favored left foot and dinking it over the keeper; he followed it up in the 50th minute by scoring an insane 360-degree header, which left the defenders, keeper, and his own teammates in awe. He even followed up his brace by providing an assist to Minamino in the 53rd minute. At this point, Haaland was performing very well in the league and had constantly put his name on the score sheet as a match day ritual. Haaland started each game hungry for goals. He scored a goal against Admira Wacker in a 5-0 thriller, which saw Salzburg take home the win and the three points. RB Salzburg faced Wattens in an away game on the 7th match day of the season. The team went in strong just as they had been doing in the previous matches and defeated the home side in a humiliating 5-1 win. Haaland was on the score sheet that day. He scored when he received the ball just inside the box and unleashed a powerful strike at the near post, which left the keeper standstill. On the 14th of September, Haaland scored a hat-trick of hat-tricks. The goals came against Hartberg in a huge 7-2 win at the Red Bull Arena. Before he got his hat-trick in the game, he had set up two of his teammates, adding two more assists to his name as well. His first goal was finished in his favorite bottom left corner, followed by an acrobatic back-heel flick, which he scored from off the floor. An odd attempt but one which showcases the lengths he'd go to get the goal! Haaland completed the hat-trick by passing the ball between the keeper's legs and straight into the goal, another one of his preferred finishing styles. The hat-trick in the fixture accounted for 11 of the goals he has scored and this was his 6th consecutive game of making the score sheet, proving the goalscoring prowess he possessed.

Although Haaland's goals would slow down in the league, his UEFA Champions League tally was just warming up. Just three days after scoring a hat-trick in the league, Haaland scored his first hat-trick in the UCL and his fourth of the season against Genk. All three of his goals came in the first half, a game where Salzburg would go on to win 6 - 2. The next fixtures in Europe were against two of the top teams in Europe and their respective countries, Liverpool and Napoli. Haaland went on to score against Liverpool at their home ground of Anfield. Minamino's pass broke through three defenders and fell kindly to Haaland who nudged it in the empty net. He then went on to score a brace against Napoli, a penalty followed by a thumping header. These goals made Haaland the second teenager to score in his first three UEFA Champions League appearances, second only to Karim Benzema. However, he was first when it comes to the number of goals scored in the first three matches, which was 6. He then scored yet another penalty against Napoli in the reverse fixture, making him the fourth player of any age to achieve such feat. Haaland's name was put up among great players such as Ze Carlos, Allesandro Del Piero, and Diego Costa. He was still the first teenager to score in the first four games of the UCL though. He then went back to his scoring ways in the league by scoring one past Rapid Wien in their tight 3-2 win and put a further three points past Wolfsberger to record his fifth hat-trick of the season. Haaland was the lone scorer against Wolfsberger on the 10th of November, taking Salzburg to a 3-0 win; this was also his second hat-trick against their opponent.

Erling Haaland returned to the UCL as hungry as ever, coming off the bench on the 27th of November to score against Genk, putting him amongst the greats such as Robert Lewandowski, Cristiano Ronaldo, Del Piero, and Neymar to score a goal in their first five matches in the UCL group stage. He was also the first teenager amongst these to have scored on all 5 initial games. He returned to the Austrian Bundesliga to score early on in the 9th minute by sliding into the ball with his right foot. During this time, there was no surprise when big clubs started enquiring about Haaland's details. It was only a matter of time before someone came knocking. His insane goalscoring record, matched with an eye for goal, is something every club looks out for in a potent striker.

Salzburg faced Liverpool in the reverse fixture of the UCL, where a win would potentially help them advance in the competition. However, Haaland and his teammates succumbed to a 2-0 defeat by The Reds and were eliminated from the competition. Despite not scoring in that game, all eyes were still on him. As the winter transfer window drew closer, clubs began approaching the wonder kid to bring him aboard their respective clubs. This would later prove to be true, and the loss to Liverpool would be Haaland's final game with Red Bull Salzburg.

He had a lucrative yet short run with the club, having scored 29 goals for the club, of which 28 goals came in the 2018/2019 season in which he played just 22 matches for the Austrian Giant. Despite departing in the winter transfer window, Erling Braut Haaland remained Salzburg's top goalscorer in all competitions with 28 goals, all of which helped the team secure their 10th consecutive league title in his absence. Salzburg even went on to win the Austrian Cup, thrashing their opponent 5 - 0 in the final.

Haaland, on the other hand, was being heavily negotiated for and monitored by clubs, such as Manchester United, which is now managed by Ole Gunnar Solskjaer, Haaland's former manager at Molde FK. Other clubs such as Juventus and Borussia Dortmund were also after the superstar.

# TAKING HIS TALENTS TO GERMANY: BORUSSIA DORTMUND

Ultimately, it was the Black and Yellow that confirmed the signing of the young Norwegian on the 29th of December 2019. Borussia Dortmund was so fast into the deal that they signed him 3 days before the start of the winter transfer window. Erling agreed to a 4 and a half year deal with Borussia Dortmund, who paid a fee of around €20+ Million for his services.

It was later reported that Borussia Dortmund signed the well-regarded youth talent, Erling Braut Haaland, from Red Bull Salzburg, by paying a large sum of €22.5 Million, which triggered his release clause set by the Austrian giants in his initial contract. The contract which Borussia Dortmund offered had more attached to it rather than just the release clause. For example, the young 19-year-old's agent, Mino Raiola, who is an elite agent for many high-profile players under his guidance, would receive a €10 million commission fee or payment on top of the existing release clause triggered by the BVB.

The German club was very lucky to have acquired Erling Haaland, as the Norwegian Teenager had gained quite the hype and attention, which linked him to a lot of top English Premier League and high-profile European clubs. He signed the contract with the Black and Yellows, which will last until the 30th of June 2024. This shows that the German side isn't willing to let go of their newly acquired prospect early or cheap with rumors claiming that a large release clause was added to his contract. The contract also stated that Borussia Dortmund will owe an undisclosed percentage to Haaland's previous club, Red Bull Salzburg, if any future sale happens and Haaland leaves Signal Iduna Park. With a list of clubs still monitoring his every move, yet another big money transfer may be on the horizon for Haaland.

Amongst the top European and English clubs showing interest in the Norwegian is Manchester United, which could have brought him on board in the Premier League. With current manager Ole Gunnar Solskjaer reuniting with his young prospect from Molde FK, Ole has publicly stated that he regularly communicates with the golden boy. United could have brought him in with the help of Ole, as he played a vital role in bringing Haaland to Molde and giving him the opportunity he deserved. United did thoroughly scout the 19-year-old Norwegian international on multiple occasions; however, they faced tons of pressure from European giants such as Real Madrid, Juventus, Barcelona, Manchester City, Atletico, Bayern Munchen, Chelsea, and Arsenal. All these clubs had shown keen interest in the player, going as far as to scout him for an extended period of time. Overall, nearly 20 clubs had shown real interest in getting Haaland to join their clubs.

Manchester United, despite being front runners in the Haaland race, slowly put brakes on the idea after having a meeting with Haaland's agent, Mino Raiola, and the player's father, Alf Inge Haaland. In the meeting, demands made by the player's party cooled down any jump the Manchester giants were willing to make, as the proposed demands contained a clause where any future or potential transfer would result in a percentage of the transfer fee and similarly with the buyout clause set in place. United did not approve of the demands and, therefore, the deal fell short.

Borussia Dortmund took the opportunity and presented a revised contract offer, which both parties agreed to. Borussia Dortmund's CEO, Hans-Joachim Watzke, publicly stated that:

"Despite interest from many other top clubs in Europe, Erling Haaland has opted for the sporting challenge that BVB is able to offer as well as the opportunities we presented him with. Our persistence has paid off."

The Club's very own Sporting Director, Michael Zorc, added to the statement made by the CEO, saying:

"We can all look forward to welcoming an ambitious, athletic, and physically strong center forward who has a nose for goal as well as impressive pace. We want to improve him as a player at Dortmund. At 19 years of age, he is, of course, still at the beginning of what will hopefully be a glittering career!"

The statements clearly reflect the desire of the team to have Haaland on board not only for monetary value but as a player they wish to see grow in their facilities. Their nonstop persuasion and persistent attempts later secured the deal.

Haaland scored 17 goals in just 16 league appearances for Salzburg after joining from Molde in January – as well as eight goals in six Champions League matches.

Haaland was one of the top if not the top hottest property in modern football. When you rack up 17 goals in 16 games as he did for Salzburg right after transitioning from a completely different team and league, such as Molde FK, that speaks for itself. Haaland joined his former club in the Austrian league at the start of the New Year in January. He then proceeded to score 8 goals in 6 UEFA Champions League appearances, breaking multiple records and joining the greats for his feat.

Erling Haaland, the son of an experienced Premier league defensive midfielder, Alf Inge Haaland, went on to say this about his decision and his new venture with the club.

"I had the feeling that I definitely wanted to transfer to this club, take this path and play in the incredible atmosphere that Dortmund provides in front of more than 80,000 spectators. I literally cannot wait to get started."

The club, Borussia Dortmund, soon released a statement about the player, including when he would join his new teammates on training and match days. The club added that Erling Haaland will join his team and teammates in the first week of January, later stating 3rd January as the exact date. After uniting with the team, Haaland will join them to travel to Marbella, Spain for a special training camp held by the club, which was scheduled the following day on the 4th of January 2020.

Erling Haaland, after spending roughly 3 weeks with the club and teammates, was eligible and fit to make his Bundesliga debut, facing a new upcoming challenge in Germany. A lot of expectations and eyes were on the young lad. He was included in the lineup against FC

Augsburg on the 18th of January 2020 but was not listed as a starter. Dortmund was not having the best of starts or half, as they were 1-0 down at the break, with no sign of Haaland coming on after the break. Augsburg capitalized twice despite Julian Brandt pulling one back for BVB. Haaland was brought on in the 56th minute of the game after Augsburg had just expanded their lead to 3 - 1.

Within 3 minutes of coming on, Haaland made a decisive run and put the ball at the back of the net, scoring his first goal for BVB against Augsburg. It was a thunderous start to his Dortmund career—3 minutes, 1 touch, and 1 goal. A long ball from deep set up Jaden Sancho, allowing Dortmund to score yet another goal, tying the score at 3 - 3. The comeback was complete but the Black and Yellow weren't finished. In the 70th minute, Thorgan Hazard and Erling Haaland broke in behind the defense. Hazard cut the ball in after dribbling the keeper and passed the ball to Erling Haaland who tapped it in to complete the comeback and his brace in a thrilling debut game. Nine minutes later, in the 79th minute a through ball to Haaland saw him outpace the Augsburg defense to score his third goal of the match, sealing his first Bundesliga hat-trick on his debut and put the game to bed. Haaland had completed his hat-trick in a span of just 23 minutes. This feat made him the only other player, aside from Pierre Emerick Aubameyang, to score a hat-trick on their Bundesliga debut.

Erling Haaland had cemented his presence in the Bundesliga and opened his ever so hefty account for the season once again. His next appearance came against local rivals, FC Koln, on the 24th of January at home in the Signal Iduna Park—his first appearance in front of the illustrious home crowd. The team had started off the match very well and had maintained a 3 - 0 lead over the rivals until Koln pulled one back in the 64th minute. Soon after, Thorgan Hazard was subbed off for the Golden Boy and the home crowd finally got to see him in action.

The team launched a quick-fire attack on the Koln defense. With three players in the box, Jaden Sancho took a shot, which was parried away toward Erling Haaland who quickly pounced on the ball and scored his first goal against a rival team at his new home ground. Just 10 minutes later, in the 87th minute, Jaden Sancho released a through ball to Haaland, who outran the defense with one touch, beat the keeper with another, stopped the ball just on the line, and curled one in from the line to score a brace. Haaland helped Dortmund overcome their rivals in a crushing 5-1 win at Signal Iduna Park. Erling Haaland soon became the first-ever Bundesliga player to score 5 goals in his first two matches. He also became the fastest player to reach a tally of 5 goals with only 56 minutes played. The superstar and Dortmund's super-sub, despite barely playing an hour in his first month with the club, was awarded Bundesliga's Player of The Month for January. His superb form and explosive arrival at the German league had all the remaining heads turning at his brilliance, breaking records, and receiving an award for playing less than an hour of football in the top flight.

Erling Haaland was roaring and ready to go for the upcoming fixture against Union Berlin on the 1st of February 2020. He was listed in the starting lineup for the first time since his arrival and did not disappoint. Dortmund was already in the lead with some individual brilliance by Jaden Sancho in the 13th minute of the match. In the 18th minute of the game, Julian Brandt launched a beautiful ball into the box, which was finished superbly by Erling Haaland, putting his name on the score sheet once again. He was later brought down in the box in the 68th minute of the game, which resulted in a penalty in favor of Dortmund. The penalty was converted by captain Marco Reus. Axel Witsel followed it up with yet another goal to put the game to bed as Dortmund now led 4 - 0. However, Haaland was not done for the day. Julian Brandt once again set up Haaland in a prime position to which he buried the ball to secure a brace and put BVB 5 - 0 up against Union Berlin. Haaland broke yet another record by becoming the first player to score 7 goals in their first 3 were to face Paris Saint-German in the Bundesliga. Erling Haaland failed to score in his 4th consecutive game, however, he came back to the pitch on the 14th of February to redeem himself once again. Haaland scored in the 54th minute via an amazing team goal, further elevating his tally to 8 goals in five Bundesliga appearances. BVB went on to win the game 4 - 0 against Frankfurt.

Borussia Dortmund had previously qualified for the next round of the UEFA Champions League before the arrival of Erling Haaland. On 18th February, Dortmund was to face Paris Saint-German in the first leg of the round of 16. The rough match saw multiple fouls and yellow cards being handed out to both teams. In the 69th minute, Haaland took a lanky touch inside the box and thumped the ball into the roof of the goal to give Dortmund the lead. He followed up his first UEFA Champions League goal by celebrating in a meditation pose. Neymar and PSG were quick to respond and soon scored the equalizer in the 75th minute through a simple tap in executed by Neymar Jr.

Haaland quickly responded in the 77th minute right after kick-off with an absolutely world-class strike from outside the box—one touch to shift the ball to his left foot and the next was an unstoppable rocket in the top left-hand corner to cancel out Neymar's goal and give Dortmund the upper hand once again. This brace in the UCL brought Haaland's European tally to 10 goals in only 8 appearances in the competition. However, PSG responded well in the reverse fixture and eliminated Haaland's Dortmund from the competition, his second exit for the same exact reason.

Haaland returned to the Bundesliga after his sensational brace against PSG and put yet another league goal past Werder Bremen on the 22nd of February. Following the match and two further fixtures, the world was put to a standstill due to the Covid-19 outbreak. Bundesliga returned behind closed doors on the 16th of May against Schalke-04, with Haaland ready to fire on all cylinders. He scored the first goal of the game in the 29th minute. It was his 10th goal of the season, which also happened to be the first goal scored in the German Professional Football League since it was halted. Dortmund went on to win the match 4-0 in yet another classic game. Later, Borussia Dortmund played against Fortuna Dusseldorf on the 13th of June 2020. The heated and close match saw no goals but plenty of yellow cards going both ways on the pitch. In the end, it was Erling Haaland who scored the game's only goal in the 95th minute, five minutes into extra time with no more time left. Akanji lifted the ball in with only a few seconds to spare. Haaland then leaped and rose to the occasion, heading the ball past the keeper to secure three points for Dortmund. On the 20th of June, a week after Haaland's winner in the league, BVB faced Red Bull Leipzig in the second last fixture of the game. The rescheduled match played at the Red Bull Arena captivated Erling Haaland. Giovanni Reyna, on his first start for the club, provided a perfect assist for Haaland who scored the first goal of the match in the 30th minute. The game was done and dusted in the 93rd minute when Julian Brandt shot the ball across the face of the goal. Erling Haaland took advantage and lunged into the ball to score a brace. The two goals scored by Haaland against Red Bull Leipzig pushed Dortmund to the 2nd spot on the league table and in perfect position for Champions League football the following season.

Erling Haaland concluded his immaculate 2019/2020 season with 44 club goals in just 40 appearances, averaging 1.1 goals per game played for both Salzburg and Dortmund. The BVB placed 3 points higher than RB Leipzig on the league table to secure the UCL spot as Bayern Munich comfortably sat on top with a 13-point lead. The only silverware Dortmund lifted that season was at the start, when they beat Bayern Munich to the DFL Super Cup in August of 2019, way before the arrival of Erling Haaland. At this point in time, Erling Braut Haaland was making big waves and receiving constant media attention—all the hype and praises from great players before him. His breakthrough was inevitable; however, he wasn't ready to move on just quick. Haaland was still very much developing as a player at Dortmund with ample game time; his young age, although a positive, maybe looked down upon when playing value is brought into the equation, something that Haaland cares about dearly. His 16 goals in 18 games for Dortmund were just a few off the club's top scorer, Jaden Sancho, that season. Explosive pace, strong build, close control, accurate finishing, imminent positioning, and overall strong mentality are what make Haaland a beast. Though his intention to stay at Dortmund was made clear, teams still enquire about him.

The 2020-2021 season kicked off on the 19th of September when Borussia Dortmund hosted Borussia Monchengladbach at Signal Iduna Park for the first game of the season. A sense of normality returned with the new season, as 10,000 fans were allowed in the stadium to cheer on the home team. The battle of the Borussias kicked off with intense support and new hopes for either team. The first goal of the game, courtesy of Gio Reyna, was his first goal for BVB. In the second half, Giovanni Reyna was caught inside the penalty box. After the VAR check, Dortmund was awarded a penalty kick. Haaland towered over the ball in the 54th minute, slotting the ball in the left-hand side and sending the keeper the wrong way. Haaland got his first-ever penalty goal in the Bundesliga and further opened his account for the season, with Dortmund comfortably in the lead. A rare statistic was released about Dortmund and Haaland, which stated that Dortmund has never lost a Bundesliga game in which Haaland was on the scoresheet. Jaden Sancho's run in the 77th minute ended with a pass to Haaland in front of goal, who finished it over the keeper to secure the match for the BVB. The game ended in a 3-0 victory for Dortmund as Haaland got his first brace of the season. Dortmund faced title contenders, Bayern Munich, in the DFL-Supercup on the 30th of September in a fierce rivalry known as the Der Klassiker. Haaland scored the equalizer in that game, which was not enough as Bayern got away with a 2 - 3 win. Haaland continued his goalscoring spree in the Bundesliga, scoring a brace against Freiburg in the 3rd match day of the season and another goal against Schalke in their 3-0 win at home. On the 7th of November, the Black and Yellows again faced Bayern Munchen, this time in the Bundesliga. The match proceeded in a similar manner to their previous encounter in the season with Erling Haaland scoring but ultimately losing 2 - 3 in the match.

The second defeat to Bayern had awakened Haaland as their next league encounter with Hertha BSC away would prove to be a lively match for the Norwegian. In just 32 minutes of the game, Haaland had scored 4 goals against the side as Dortmund went on to win 2 - 5. Dortmund was down by 1 goal at halftime when Cunha struck an unbelievable strike to give Hertha a 1-0 lead. Haaland got his first goal right after the halftime whistle as Emre Can played a ball across goal in the 47th minute, which was tapped in by the young Norwegian. Two minutes later, Haaland made it 2 for himself and 2 for Dortmund as they now lead the tie 1-2. He capitalized on a defensive mistake in the 62nd minute to complete the hat-trick, his first of the season. A decisive run through the middle of the defenders granted Haaland his 4th goal of the night in the 79th minute, finally putting the game to bed in a 2-5 thriller. The 5 goals scored by Erling Haaland in November crowned him the Bundesliga Player of the Month for the second time in his career.

Erling Haaland continued his hot streak of scoring goals in the UCL as he bagged 6 goals in Dortmund's opening 4 matches in the competition. His brace against Club Brugge in the group stage made him the fastest player to score 15 and then 16 goals in the competition having only made just 12 appearances. Haaland would later suffer a hamstring injury, which would keep him out until the start of the New Year.

Haaland made his timely return on the 3rd of January 2021 against Wolfsburg. He did not score upon his return, but he scored a brace against Red Bull Leipzig just 6 days later to account for goals he hadn't scored while he was injured. He scored yet another brace against Borussia Monchengladbach. However, his side lost 4-2. He was then decisive against Sevilla on the 17th of February in their 3-2 away win, scoring two and providing an assist for the other goal in the first leg of the round of 16. The brace brought his UCL tally up to 18 goals in just 13 games. On the 6th of March 2021, Borussia Dortmund would now face Bayern Munich in the reverse fixture, with Haaland looking for revenge. Haaland opened the scoring and then bagged in another one before halftime to get his brace within 10 minutes. His brace against Bayern brought his tally up to 100 senior career goals, a feat he achieved in just 146 games. Haaland was later subbed off during the half as he suffered a knock. Bayern turned the tie around in the second half winning the game 4-2. The reverse UCL fixture against Sevilla came about on the 9th of March, where Haaland proved decisive once again by scoring a brace, as their side drew the game 2-2 but advanced to the quarterfinals. With only 14 appearances in the competition, Haaland broke a record for reaching the 20-goal milestone. He was the fastest player and the youngest player in the history of the competition to do so. He also broke a record for scoring multiple goals in four back-to-back matches.

Currently just 20 years of age, Haaland is no doubt one of the best or the best young player in the world. He has accumulated many awards and honors on his journey to becoming the greatest, most notably winning the Golden

Boy award in 2020, which signified his importance and potential as a superstar. He was also later named in the FIFA FIFPro World11, following his amazing performance in the year 2020. He was also awarded the Gullballen and Kniksen Honor Awards, which are given to the Best Norwegian footballer.

# MORE FROM JACKSON CARTER BIOGRAPHIES

My goal is to spark the love of reading in young adults around the world. Too often children grow up thinking they hate reading because they are forced to read material they don't care about. To counter this we offer accessible, easy to read biographies about sportspeople that will give young adults the chance to fall in love with reading.

## Go to the Website Below to Join Our Community

https://mailchi.mp/7cced1339ff6/jcbcommunity

## Or Find Us on Facebook at

www.facebook.com/JacksonCarterBiographies

## As a Member of Our Community You Will Receive:

First Notice of Newly Published Titles

Exclusive Discounts and Offers

Influence on the Next Book Topics

Don't miss out, join today and help spread the love of reading around the world!

# OTHER WORKS BY JACKSON CARTER BIOGRAPHIES

Patrick Mahomes: The Amazing Story of How Patrick Mahomes Became the MVP of the NFL

Donovan Mitchell: How Donovan Mitchell Became a Star for the Salt Lake City Jazz

Luka Doncic: The Complete Story of How Luka Doncic Became the NBA's Newest Star

The Eagle: Khabib Nurmagomedov: How Khabib Became the Top MMA Fighter and Dominated the UFC

Lamar Jackson: The Inspirational Story of How One Quarterback Redefined the Position and Became the Most Explosive Player in the NFL

Jimmy Garoppolo: The Amazing Story of How One Quarterback Climbed the Ranks to Be One of the Top Quarterbacks in the NFL

Zion Williamson: The Inspirational Story of How Zion Williamson Became the NBA's First Draft Pick

Kyler Murray: The Inspirational Story of How Kyler Murray Became the NFL's First Draft Pick

Do Your Job: The Leadership Principles that Bill Belichick and the New England Patriots Have Used to Become the Best Dynasty in the NFL

Turn Your Gaming Into a Career Through Twitch and Other Streaming Sites: How to Start, Develop and Sustain an Online Streaming Business that Makes Money

From Beginner to Pro: How to Become a Notary Public

Printed in Great Britain
by Amazon

64972906R00031